I0087212

JOHN CORTESE

# THE PARENTS GUIDE TO
# STRENGTH AND CONDITIONING
## — FOR SPORTS —

## JOHN CORTESE

# TABLE OF CONTENTS

CHAPTER ONE
# Introduction

So many kids today are involved in sports activities, and that's a great thing! Our young people need to move, to stay active, in order to develop healthy habits for the rest of their lives.

My job as a trainer is to help those young athletes achieve their greatest potential. This book is for parents who are looking to help their son or daughter develop that athletic edge for their sports.

Parents want to see their children do the best they can, and part of that is having a good experience in the activities they participate in. I'm going to help you weed out all the misinformation that is out there and give you the honest truth about what you really need to be looking for to help your young athlete develop into the best he or she can be.

Why do you need what I'm here to tell you? You've heard the old saying: Knowledge is power. Knowledge from someone who has many years of experience gives you an advantage to make educated decisions about your child's athletic future. You want to seek advice from someone who can guide you in the right direction so you don't make the same mistakes that maybe others have made.

A young athlete can train in the right way or the wrong way. My guidance will save you time, money, and frustration—save you from all the hassles of having to learn as you go—because you'll be doing it right from the very beginning. You won't just be spinning your wheels and feeling like there's nowhere to turn.

It's very important for parents to understand that they have someone to turn to who can be a useful resource when they're looking to get their children into a training program or athletic program.

## WHO IS JOHN CORTESE?

Before we go any further, I think it's important for you to understand who I am and what my qualifications are. I have a very long background in this field. I've been immersed in youth athletics since I was about 13 years old, and I have always been extremely interested in the field of human performance and athletic development since I was that age. Through my own hard work, I came to understand that whatever you put in is what you get out.

I was a two-sport athlete for ten years. I played football and ran track all the way through the collegiate level. I graduated from California Polytechnic State University, San Luis Obispo with a degree in Exercise Science, and I've been in the strength and conditioning field as a professional since I was 21 years old. However, it's been my absolute passion since my early teens.

I'm here to help any serious athlete or parent of an athlete get to the next level. Even if the athlete is not actually "serious" but just wants to understand how the body works and how being strong and fit is important for overall health throughout life, I can help out.

I own and operate a strength and conditioning business in Napa, California, where my staff and I train youth, middle school, high school, and collegiate athletes. Most of my clients are kids who are involved in sports, wanting to do something extra to help improve their overall athletic performance.

## WHAT PARENTS WILL LEARN FROM THIS BOOK

After reading this book, parents are going to have a much better understanding of what it takes to see success in helping their children reach their athletic goals and that it's really not as complicated as some people make it out to be. I understand that team sports are very busy. There are a lot of practices and meetings and then, of course, the actual games that go along with it, but it's important to understand that it doesn't take a whole lot of extra time per week to train for athletic performance. It does, however, take consistency and continuous training over the years.

I want parents to understand that training is actually safe and beneficial for their kids, especially when done correctly in a supervised, professional environment, which we'll get into in more detail. It's also very important, for anyone who is involved in a sport to take care of his or her body, both mentally and physically. A sports performance program such as ours develops a more well rounded athlete. It's like anything—if you try to train on your own, you're going to spend much more time trying to get the job done with most likely minimal results than if you seek the help from a professional. A professional can help speed up that learning curve and provide much quicker results.

If you need to run faster, jump higher, and get stronger for your sport, CTS can help. Call us directly at (707) 738-0190 to discuss how we can help your son or daughter become the best athlete they can be.

CHAPTER TWO
# The Benefits of Strength Training for Sports

When young people come to me for help with their athletic performance, the first thing I recommend is strength training. Strength training has a number of benefits for sports.

## THE MENTAL ASPECT

I think the first thing that strength training does for young athletes is to make them more confident in themselves. All of a sudden they're doing things in the gym that they thought were maybe impossible. We post a lot of pictures in the gym of clients, and you'll hear a young person say, "Oh, I'll never be able to do that!"

And then, after they've done some strength training, they discover that they can do the same thing! That's a real confidence booster. These kids start feeling better about themselves, which ties into self-esteem. Before you know it, they perceive themselves as a totally different person. Six months ago, maybe they were this shy, timid kid. Now, they've transformed into this strong, confident person, and it's just a drastic transformation.

A second part of this transformation is that strength training increases mental toughness. Again, these kids start training, and all of a sudden, they're being asked to do things that are going to challenge their mental toughness. There are certain things they are not going to want to do, but it's always for their benefit. We're always looking out for their best interest and their well-being, and they're going to find that their confidence, mental toughness, and self-esteem increase tremendously.

## INJURY PREVENTION

As you get stronger, your mobility and flexibility improves. Another added benefit from strength training is injury prevention.

We watch professional athletes every week get injured, and for parents, it can be scary. Parents want to ensure the safety of their children as much as possible. One way to do that is through strength training.

Obviously, you can't predict when injuries will occur, and you can't completely eliminate them from sports activities, but you can definitely prepare your body to be as resilient and as strong as possible. That's going to reduce the risk of a non-contact-related injury. For example, if a basketball player goes up for a rebound, comes down, and then he blows an ACL because of lack of physical preparation, that kind of thing can be prevented. Or if a soccer player goes after a ball and makes a quick cut in the grass, and her foot goes one way while her knee goes the other, which happens all the time, again, that can be a preventable injury.

Most of the time, injuries in sports like softball and baseball come from overuse, from too much repetition of the same skill over and over, without adequate physical preparation for the sport. That's absolutely going to lead to injuries, but these injuries are preventable, and strength training will help a lot with longevity in the sport.

Incorporating an additional strength training program is also going to help with enjoyment of the sport. Simply put, if a player is injured, he's most likely not going to have the most enjoyable experience.

He's going to dread playing again, and eventually he might get burned out altogether. It's one of those things where a little prevention in the form of strength training can help with an athlete's entire attitude toward playing.

A lot of these kids—and some parents, as well—think, "It's not going to happen to me." I understand where they're coming from, but you never know when something might happen. It's in an athlete's best interest to prepare as much as possible so that you don't see an unnecessary injury happening to your son or daughter. The last thing we'd want is a preventable injury that could limit future opportunities for the athlete. That's why I think it's very important to look at strength training as part of an injury-prevention strategy.

## REDUCING ACL TEARS

One injury that plagues athletes of all ages and all skill levels is tearing the anterior cruciate ligament (ACL) in the knee. I think that ACL tears can be reduced by simply focusing on getting stronger through multiple means of movement and direction. In other words, it's not sufficient anymore for an athlete just to play his or her sport. Athletes have to be very well rounded. Some sports are very movement-dominant in one plane of movement. For example, in a sport like soccer, where you see a very high incidence of ACL injuries, there's a lot of slow movement in between repeated bursts for the ball and a lot of change of direction. Sudden change of direction places a high amount of force on the joints, and if the athlete is not physically prepared, the muscles of the legs and hips cannot absorb force, as they should. This is when injury occurs. What we're seeing is more sports that require athletes to be very strong in order to absorb that force on their joints.

I think that if parents and athletes would focus on developing general strength throughout their bodies and through multiple planes of movement, ACL tears would be dramatically reduced. This will be true especially if you treat training as a year-round program. It can't be just for four to six weeks before the season. You have to look at training as year-round maintenance, just like you take care of your car. You can't just change your oil once and call it good. It has to be taken care of year-round; otherwise, it's going to break down.

It's the same with your body. An athlete has to take care of themself all the time, and it's got to be treated seriously. If your young athlete tears an ACL, he or she is going to have surgery, and the recovery and comeback take a long time. In addition, athletic performance may never be the same again. So it's very important to do everything you can to prevent those injuries from occurring.

## PHYSICAL IMPROVEMENTS

Strength training does more than boost confidence and prevent injuries, though. It can drastically improve performance on the field of play.

The number-one request I hear from parents regarding the performance of their son(s) and/or daughter(s) is that they want them to get faster. They want their young athletes to have more speed. Coupled with that is the quality that builds speed or power—strength. I think that one of the main benefits of strength training is that it indirectly helps to improve the athlete's speed.

As an athlete gets stronger, his muscles can contract harder and produce more force. Basically, the muscles are responding to the ground. The increased force produced by that muscle is going to put more force into the ground. In turn, the athlete will have an opposite reaction to that force, which indirectly translates into running faster. It's not going to magically happen overnight because it's got to be consistent and year-round. But everybody— and I mean everybody—who improves their overall strength is going to be able to jump higher and run faster. They're going to get more power and more speed just by getting stronger.

As an example, strength is like the foundation of a house. When you have a strong foundation for your house, your house is going to be able to withstand the elements much better. The stronger the athlete's foundation, the more overall strength the athlete has, the more potential they have to run faster and jump higher. He or she will also have better posture, fewer injuries, better balance, and more coordination—all qualities that are going to help with athletic performance.

## THE FIVE P'S

To quote the great NFL linebacker Ray Lewis, "Proper preparation prevents poor performance." Preparation is vital to ensure that a child performs to the best of his or her abilities. If you're playing a sport, you want to be as prepared as possible. The more you prepare your body in the offseason, the more you'll be confident when it comes time to play and the less you'll have to worry about whether or not you're ready. That's opposed to somebody who waits until the last minute to prepare—and is frantically trying to fit in as much training as possible before the season starts.

The athlete who has been training year-round is ready. No freaking out, no stress, no worry. Those athletes know what they've done in the offseason and throughout the year, and they're ready to go.

It's a seamless transition, like nothing has changed; it's part of their lifestyle, part of their daily routine.

So I think it's very important to understand that the more prepared you are, the easier it's going to be when it's game time. This transitions into life in general. Being athletically prepared teaches these kids how to prepare for life and how to manage their time. It shows them that the more you prepare and the more you have a healthy lifestyle and routine, your life will become much more structured and much less chaotic in the end.

It's also important to understand that these specific qualities like speed and power and strength take a long time to develop. You can't possibly see maximum results over the short period of time, say for instance, in six to eight weeks. You can achieve good results in a short amount of time, but the likelihood that those results will stick is pretty low.

You also have to understand that it's about enjoying the journey. It's a never-ending process; it's not just about focusing on the end result. So it's important to be very aware of simply enjoying the ride, having fun, taking it day to day, and trying to get better over time.

If you need to run faster, jump higher, and get stronger for your sport, CTS can help. Call us directly at (707) 738-0190 to discuss how we can help your son or daughter become the best athlete they can be.

CHAPTER THREE

# Myths about Strength Training for Sports

I said it before—knowledge is power. There's a lot of information out there about youth athletics, training, the best methods, and so forth. Some of that information is accurate and relevant, and some is not. Some of this information is really confusing when it comes to strength training, especially as it relates to sports. I know that parents hear this information, these myths, and may be hesitant to start their kids in a strength training program. I'll address some of these myths one by one.

## "STRENGTH TRAINING MAKES YOU SLOWER."

This myth has been passed along for many years. I think it's because some people, when they think of "strength training," they think of this bulky body-builder type of person, like you see on the cover of a magazine. They automatically think, "My child is going to look like this person." They see these people in the media, in TV shows, in the movies, and they're so large that they can barely move, so people think, "Well, it must be that the more muscle you have, the less flexibility you have." Therefore, you're not going to be able to move very well on the field.

Let me tell you that the way an athlete trains is different from the way a bodybuilder trains. An athlete is not training for looks; an athlete is training for performance.

For athletic performance, we break down strength training by movements, and by training movement patterns. You build functional movement for the athletes, and you train for functional strength. "Functional strength" is a term that is badly overused in this field, but it helps for parents to understand that if you train the athletes in specific movement patterns, we're actually teaching them how to use their body as one unit. The body works together as a whole. If you can train as many muscles as possible to fire explosively all at once, you'll produce a lot of force at the same time and have a very dominant athlete.

That's the type of strength training that we use for athletics. It's important to remember what you're training for. Bodybuilders train for looks; athletes train for performance first and foremost. The strength training that athletes use always has the end result in mind of "Is this going to make me better? Is this going to make me more powerful? Is this going to make me faster?" And the answer is yes, without a doubt. And if you can produce more force than the other athletes you're playing against, you're going to be faster than they are. All other things being equal, this is a big differentiator that can set you apart.

## "STRENGTH TRAINING MAKES FEMALE ATHLETES BULKY."

I understand this concern completely. Parents want their daughters to maintain a feminine appearance. They don't want her looking like a linebacker! But at the same time, they want her to be a strong athlete.

Parents need to know a couple of things. First, and most importantly, women just do not produce the amount of testosterone that males do. And it's testosterone that helps men bulk up. The same sex hormone that makes the voice deeper and produces body and facial hair is responsible for big, bulky muscles. Females, on the other hand, produce much more estrogen than men, so they're estrogen-dominant rather than testosterone-dominant.

Female athletes certainly benefit and perform well with strength training. Every human is going to be able to build muscle. But females are going to put it on a little bit differently. They're not going to gain as much muscle mass as men and therefore will be less likely to gain as much weight from strength training. They will, however, lose body fat and also see tremendous increases in injury prevention. Many female athletes don't typically get involved in strength training programs, and for this reason, I think many of them are prone to injury.

Finally, they're simply going to feel better about themselves. They're going to be lean and healthy, but they're not going to look like a guy. It's just physically impossible, physiologically. If young women are afraid of weight gain, they should know that muscle burns calories much faster than fat, so weight gain from muscle mass won't be a problem if their diet is balanced and they're training hard.

You may say, "Now, wait a minute, John, I've seen

those female bodybuilders. How do they get big?"
It's true that a woman can build muscle mass like
that under very specific conditions. It's purposeful
and planned by ollowing a strict diet and eating
regime, and training in a very specific way designed
to build mass. This is not the norm, just like male
bodybuilders are not the norm for men who
strength train. The bottom line is that female
athletes need strength training. It's absolutely
essential if they want to be the best athelete they
can be. And no, they won't look like the boys!

## "STRENGTH TRAINING STUNTS YOUR GROWTH."

For some reason, there's a stereotype in the
media of the short, stocky weight lifter with all these
muscles. This image has led to a myth that strength
training when you're younger keeps you from
growing taller.

I have to say, this is my favorite myth. It's really
funny, but unfortunately, I have to address it frequently.
I understand that parents are concerned about the
safety and health of their children.

Parents have to realize that they determine their kids' height—at the genetic level. So no matter what sport you play or what training activities you do, barring serious injury to a growth plate, which takes a tremendous amount of force, your height is going to be what it's going to be, regardless of what you do.

If anything, as I tell parents, strength training actually enhances bone growth. Strength training is a stressor on the body, but it's a good kind of stress. The body responds by developing more tissue. You may have read that women benefit from strength training because it helps to reduce the risk of osteoporosis. It's the same with young bodies; strength training helps to develop strong, more resilient bone tissue, which would heal faster in the case of a broken bone, for instance.

In fact, kids are always breaking bones, even at young ages, in team sports like football. The sports themselves pose a much greater risk to the athletes than strength training, which can only serve to make them stronger and healthier.

Strength training has the lowest injury risk per participant, as long as it's structured and supervised properly. And I've never, ever seen anybody injure a growth plate from strength training. In all the years I've been doing this, we've had zero incidence of somebody shrinking or not growing because of strength training. If kids are short, they're going to be short regardless of what they do. We've had kids that started when they were 10 years old, and they're taller than me now, six feet tall or more, and they were five-two when they started out. We had one kid who was five-nine in the eighth grade; he's trained with us ever since, and he's now 17 years old and six-foot-eight. Wow, right?

There are no documented studies that prove this idea to be true. But there are lots of studies from very reputable sources that show otherwise, that strength training does not stunt growth and in fact helps promote healthy bone and muscle growth in adolescents.

## "STRENGTH TRAINING IS UNSAFE FOR YOUTH SPORTS."

This is the big one, the one that sort of ties all the

other myths together. Some people actually believe that strength training increases injuries in athletes.

First, let me say that just about any activity can be unsafe if performed incorrectly. You can throw a baseball and injure your arm, especially if you do it wrong over the long term. You can go out and tackle somebody incorrectly in football, and can get hurt, sometimes badly injured. For anyone, if you don't have the right coaching and the right programming in any activity, there is a risk.

This myth probably got started when some young person unfortunately got injured doing strength training because **a)** he wasn't coached properly and was possibly using weight he wasn't ready for, or **b)** he was doing it on his own, without a coach at all. The thing is, if you progress the activity safely in the right way, if you start it off in kids with age-appropriate programming, then the risk of injury is low. We have kids that are 8 years old that train with us, and they've never been hurt from strength training. It prevents injury. It toughens the body.

If anything, kids' bodies are more resilient to outside contact with strength training. Kids climb up trees and jump off all the time. And nobody ever bats an eye at that. Even running, every time their foot hits the ground, is the equivalent to three to four times their body weight on each leg. So that's a lot more force on your body than a 10-pound barbell. Think about it—400 pounds of force on one leg versus 10 pounds of external weight on their back while squatting. This level of strength training presents a very minimal risk of injury, if any at all.

I've been doing this a long time, and the risk of injury is very low. Although we like to think it shouldn't happen, the chance of a young athlete getting injured in the weight room is actually extremely low when supervised and coached properly. Sometimes kids goof around with their parent's weight set in the garage, for example, trying to impress each other and things could go very wrong. In that instance the risk of injury goes up. But in a structured, professional setting with expert coaching, the chance of a young athlete getting hurt should be minimized to where one should not have any concerns.

If you need to run faster, jump higher, and get stronger for your sport, CTS can help. Call us directly at (707) 738-0190 to discuss how we can help your son or daughter become the best athlete they can be.

CHAPTER FOUR

# Fundamentals of Strength Training for Sports

The most fundamental question concerning strength training for sports is to determine the baseline of the athlete before they start. Young people need to have a foundation of bodyweight strength, balance, and general fitness first and foremost. Once these measures are addressed, I can make my recommendations and go from there.

We have certain standards that we like to see in all of our athletes. They need to be able to learn how to squat; they need to know how to do a lunge and a push-up; they need to have the basics in place. Basic programming for beginners is going to involve bodyweight work, no equipment. We worry about the fancy stuff later on down the road. There's no rush. This is a long-term journey.

## WHERE TO START

Younger athletes should start with a very age-appropriate, structured training program that has been designed by a professional. Obviously, a beginning athlete is not going to have any idea what to do. And his parents are probably wondering, where do we go?

What do we do?

Just like with any beginner, they're going to need to have their bodyweight strength in place first. They're going to need to know how to move their bodies in different planes of movement. After that, they can begin to use very light implements like light medicine balls and light barbells. It's just progressively loaded over time.

## WHAT EXERCISES TO USE

Moving your own bodyweight is the first requirement of strength training. Can you move your own body through space? Seems pretty simple right? Well you'd be amazed at the number of kids that struggle with utilizing their own bodyweight. That is the most basic kind of strength training, and it's very important. As long as your muscles are contracting and exerting force, that's resistance training.

After bodyweight exercises, the athlete can start using light equipment. We start them with medicine balls and light barbells, and then we progress by gradually adding weight to the bar over time. Then you can go to dumbbells or other equipment like bands or sleds. But I like to stick with the basics, first and foremost, bodyweight and barbells. Everything after that is pretty much icing on the cake.

## PROPER TECHNIQUE AND INSTRUCTION

We always, always, always start with the lightest and simplest form of an exercise possible. We want to break down the movement that we're teaching. Note that we typically call them "movements" rather than "exercises." We want the movements to be as simple as possible, especially for the youngest athletes, who need it to be very simple and easy to understand.

We start teaching from the most basic beginner level, and every instruction starts with safety and technique. We do not load an exercise if the athlete's technique is not up to the standard for more weight. So let's say we're teaching an athlete how to do a squat, and their heels come off the ground or knees buckle in while holding an empty barbell. We know then that that athelete is not ready to add weight to the bar because he needs to be able to keep his posture and technique right with an empty bar first. Technique and safety first. We worry about the weight later on.

A lot of times, athletes learn "technique" from a television program, on a website, or from social media. They see some guy doing it and they think they can follow suit. I believe that's why a lot of kids get injured, because they do a lot of this training on their own without receiving the proper education and instruction. That's why it's so important for young athletes to get involved with a professional training facility that is dedicated to athletic development, especially places that specialize in young athletes in this case. Kids need to have the proper preparation before they get involved in strength training.

You must teach movement the right way from the very beginning if at all possible. Otherwise, it's very difficult for a coach to undo bad habits that have developed over time. If someone has been doing the same movement for four or five years, and then comes to a coach for training but is moving poorly, it's going to be harder for the coach to fix those movement patterns than it would be if the coach had that person early on and was taught correctly from the beginning. If you learn a skill the right way from the beginning, then it's a much smoother, more seamless transition.

It's also very important to have that outside feedback because sometimes an athlete is unaware of how a movement should be performed unless a coach tells them and puts them in the right position. It's just like with anything; if you want to be the best you can possibly be, you're going to need some coaching and proper, professional feedback.

## THE RIGHT ATMOSPHERE

Kids today want to play for the best travel teams or be at the top of whatever sport they're playing. And of course, parents want their kids to play for the best. Part of that is coaching, the teammates, and the facilities where you train. That's how you build results, with atmosphere and environment.

Here's an example—you could go train in your garage by yourself, with no music, with dim lights, and hope to get something out of that. And you might think that you're having a great workout. Then, all of a sudden, you go into a facility with like-minded athletes who are all working just as hard, if not harder, than you. They have the same goals, the same aspirations, and the same dreams as you. Do you think your intensity is going to go up? Do you think your results will improve?

With coaching, it's not just about the bars and the weights and the equipment. We're providing the experience as well. You need to be surrounded with like-minded individuals for success, no matter what your goal is. Training with people like you or better, more experienced than you, is going to challenge you and bring you up to their level. For instance, we have very high standards for how we feel our athletes should conduct themselves in and outside the gym. It's not just about the weight. It's about showing up on time. It's about doing what we ask you to do. It's about being loyal to your word. It's about doing the little things that matter because that's what is going to make you different from everybody else.

If you do the same thing everyone else is doing, you're going to get the same result. But if you do something different, and you strive to be the best, you have to surround yourself with the best. I'm not saying necessarily the best athlete, but I mean the best environment conducive to creating the best version of yourself. It's so much more than just hitting the weights and going home—it's personal development. You have to get yourself in the right environment with the right mindset, the right attitude with the right coaches, and everything will fall into place. That's what we bring to the table.

## THE IMPORTANCE OF A COACH

It's really important to have an expert in your corner for long-term success. That person can keep you grounded, keep you focused, keep you motivated. Athletes get bored very quickly. A good coach can keep athletes motivated and grounded and focused on their goals.

I know that these kids have other things going on in their lives. They've got practice and homework and a social life, or they might have issues going on with friends—whatever is going on can take a toll on training. So it's our job as experts not only to provide coaching and the experience and the atmosphere, but it's also our job to keep them grounded and motivated and focused on long-term results. I always tell them:

No matter how hard this gets, no matter how bad you feel, no matter what is going on, remember why you started this in the first place. Because you have a goal, right? Maybe it's to make the varsity volleyball team next year. Maybe it's to get a college scholarship. Whatever the goal, remember why you started and keep that in the back of your mind at all times. Because if you let little things get in the way of that, you're going to look back five or ten years from now and say, "What if?" And you never want to have any regrets. No matter what you do, your high school career is going to fly by. Your college career is going to come and go in the blink of an eye. You only have a very short window of opportunity to be the best you can be, so you might as well take advantage of that now and give it everything you've got.

If you need to run faster, jump higher, and get stronger for your sport, CTS can help. Call us directly at (707) 738-0190 to discuss how we can help your son or daughter become the best athlete they can be.

CHAPTER FIVE
# Assessing the Athlete

When parents or athletes inquire about our program I of course tell them how much I appreciate their interest. I then invite them in for an assessment to determine their individual goals and where they want to be athletically. Without that information it would be like a doctor prescribing medication without knowing what's wrong with the patient. That makes it much more difficult to solve the problem. The doctor needs to assess the patient in order to determine what needs to be done in a safe and efficient manner.

It's our job to determine where an athlete is currently at, physically, mentally, and emotionally in order for us to know where that young person needs to be three, six or twelve months down the road. I need to be able to write them a program that fits their needs and goals while addressing their strengths and weaknesses. We don't just throw anyone into a program - every single person is different and unique. Nobody moves the same way.

Furthermore, some athletes may have a prior injury history, or they might have a medical issue that we need to address as far as movement goes. So there's a lot that goes into it. If we did not assess our athletes, it's like playing darts in the dark. I might hit the bulls-eye, but the chances are slim. So I need to assess every athlete 100 percent before we can get started.

The hardest part for people when they first come to the gym is to come to grips with where they are now. It might be embarrassing for them or they might feel ashamed because they feel they don't perform well in their sport—they think they're slow or they don't jump very high or they can't do many push-ups. Whatever the issue, it's just perception. That's usually just a false image they impose on themselves.

We need to be very honest and say, "The numbers don't lie. Here's where you're at. Now that we're aware of these numbers such as body weight, body fat percentage, vertical jump, etc we can build on them and continually see improvement. Everybody has to start somewhere and it's important for me as a coach to bring the parent and athlete unbiased and honest feedback. When we're all on the same page, we can effectively develop the plan of attack and begin to make progress.

## GOING THROUGH THE ASSESSMENT

Before doing anything else in the assessment, I need to get to know the parents and the athlete. Our program is very good; it works very well. But it has to be the right fit for both parties because it's not for everybody. It's for people who want to generally better themselves. So the first step is to get to know everybody, see if it's a good fit, and determine if we can help this athlete.

Once we've gotten past that step, we're going to physically assess the athlete to see how he or she moves. We'll have them warm up with some general movement. I want to see how they move forward and backward, side to side. I want to see how flexible they are. I want to see where their strength is currently. I want to see how they jump, how they can land. I just want to see all types of different athletic movements. From there, we can present what I feel would be the best plan of attack for that young person as an individual.

The plan of attack is based on each athlete's schedule, their goals, and how serious they are. If they want to get better, we always present what we feel is the honest, best way to get the job done. I'll never recommend that an athlete join our program if he or she is not ready for it. I just give honest feedback on where each athlete currently stands and then provide the best solution to solve his or her problems. If they're ready to go, then we will definitely put them on the right track!

If you need to run faster, jump higher, and get stronger for your sport, CTS can help. Call us directly at (707) 738-0190 to discuss how we can help your son or daughter become the best athlete they can be.

CHAPTER SIX
# Training Schedules

Once a young athlete is accepted into a program and has had a complete assessment, the question comes up of how often and how long training should be.

Every athlete's needs are different, but most young athletes train with me at least twice a week, and that's year-round. The ones that see the best results are training more frequently than that, only because the more you practice a skill, the better you're going to get at it. And speed and movement are skills that can be taught. They need to be practiced repeatedly. You can't just do it once every couple of weeks.

It's got to be consistent; everybody's different, but I would say on average if you can allow for it, try to find two to three hours out of your week to get it done. Just find the time. When you look at it that way, it doesn't sound as time-consuming as most people think. I know everyone has different, busy schedules and it's going to be challenging for some, but I think if you just make the time, if it's important to you and you value it, then two to three hours per week is very doable for most people.

## THE IMPORTANCE OF CONSISTENCY

Consistency is probably the most important factor in success. Maintaining a consistent schedule, whether it's two times a week or four times a week, is crucial. You have to keep up your consistency, no matter what. If you "fall off the wagon," if you miss a week because you're too tired or you make some excuse that you can't go, it's going to be even harder for you to get back on again. The likelihood of success for a young athlete is highly dependent on how consistent he or she is.

If athletes do all they can and never miss a session, I can guarantee that they are going to have the best results. The correlation is extremely high between the athletes with the greatest results in the gym and their training consistency. The ones that skip sessions or only come in every other week have to start all over again or back track, and progress is slower. It's very frustrating as a coach because the coach wants the best for the athlete. The coach has their best interests in mind, so consistency is extremely important.

## RECOVERY

Recovery is a crucial part of strength training. Just as in the other parts of your life, you have to have balance and a time to rest in strength training. You can't train all the time and beat your body up constantly without taking a break. Recovery is what allows you to come in and feel great for the next session.

If you're not taking care of your body away from the gym, you're not going to recover as fast. You're not going to be able to train as hard. So we typically recommend that most athletes take a day every other day to do some light activity between hard training sessions. They can do stretching or foam rolling or something light, as long as they're moving. I don't recommend just sitting, but light movement is good. Some athletes can train two days in a row, take a day off, and then train hard again two or three days in a row.

A day off is also good for your mind. You need to have that mental break and get away from training, just to let yourself do something different from training all the time. You don't want to burn out. I understand that training hard is important, and being consistent is important, too, but you have to have a balance and a structure in your life, just like with anything else. Maintain some sort of sanity and make it fun. Kids especially need to have those qualities in their workouts. You've got to have fun, to enjoy life, to enjoy your family and friends. Just remember to balance hard training with light days and with stretching and foam rolling on your off days.

If you need to run faster, jump higher, and get stronger for your sport, CTS can help. Call us directly at (707) 738-0190 to discuss how we can help your son or daughter become the best athlete they can be.

CHAPTER SEVEN
# Nutrition and Recovery

A big part of training is how you eat and how you recover when you're not training. This chapter takes a look at nutrition and the recovery process.

## WATER

You often see athletes carrying water with them. Water must be important to training, right? You bet that's right. Water isn't just important for training; it's important for our very survival.

I always tell people if you're sluggish or tired or fatigued, it's probably because you're dehydrated. Water is very important for mental clarity. It's important for strong muscular contractions, and it's important for preventing muscle cramps in training. Symptoms like fatigue, nausea, lightheadedness, and just generally feeling bad can probably be improved by simply drinking more water.

Most kids drink very little water, and if they do, it's only when they're exercising. They're not sipping on it all day. The ones that do, though, are the ones that feel the best. And yeah, you're probably going to make more visits to the bathroom, but it's important to stay hydrated at all times. That's simply crucial for well-being and for overall health.

So, how much water do we need? We typically recommend drinking half your body weight in ounces per day. So if an athlete weighs, say, 150 pounds, he wants to shoot for roughly a minimum of 75 fluid ounces of water per day. He'll need to drink more depending on how active he is, as well. That sounds like a lot of ounces, but the athlete should be sipping on the water all day. Especially on the days that they're doing hard training, they will go through it really quickly.

Athletes lose a lot of water during training, so it's very important for hard-training athletes to stay hydrated. Kids don't need to chug it or slam it down all at once. That's not good for them either. They just have to keep sipping it all day, and it will go quicker than you think. It's really not that hard. It just takes diligence and they have to make it a habit.

## WHAT TO EAT

There's one principle that I always like to keep in mind with training, nutrition, and recovery, and that's KISS—keep it super simple. I don't like to overanalyze things. I don't like to make it more complicated than it needs to be.

With food, especially for young athletes, the first and most important thing is to eat breakfast. If you're not eating breakfast, it's usually because you woke up too late or maybe you don't know what to make for breakfast, or you're just generally lacking the motivation to make yourself something if mom and dad don't do it. A lot of times, everybody's in a rush to get out of the house in the morning, so a young person might just grab a couple of Pop-Tarts and think, well, I'm good to go.

Pop-Tarts aren't going to cut it. You want to eat whole food that's minimally processed most of the time, if possible, food containing lots of nutrients, high in protein (lean meats, fish, egg, etc.), good carbohydrates (sweet potatoes, brown rice, etc.), healthy fats (olive oil, nut butters, etc.), fruits, and vegetables. Eat food that is simple to prepare and eat. Don't over-complicate it.

After breakfast, it's important to stay fueled throughout the day. Be sure to have a healthy lunch and dinner, as well. Eat consistently during the day. And be sure to eat immediately after training to recover. Most athletes don't realize that they should be eating right after training and don't know what to eat.

An athlete should never be hungry. If their goal is to recover from exercise, then he or she needs to keep their body fueled at all times, but that doesn't mean snacking on cookies and chips and drinking a soda during break time. Quality is important. Athletes need to look at food as a means to recover. I see this all the time. The athletes that are the most rested and the most well-fed are going to be the best, by far. They're going to feel the best; they're going to perform the best. They're going to perform better than athletes who skip breakfast and don't eat after training or only eat at dinner. Most athletes under-eat in general. My advice is to eat more, but to keep it really, really simple. Protein with each meal, eat quality fruits and vegetables, eat nutrient dense meals, and eat frequently to stay fueled.

## THE THREE S'S: SUPPLEMENTATION, SLEEP, AND STRETCHING

These three factors all play a huge role in recovery, but of all of them, the most important by far is sleep. Everybody, young athletes especially, needs to get enough sleep in order to feel their best. Sleep is when you recover the most. That's when the body regenerates. So your young person needs to be getting in bed at a decent hour. That means not staying up until 3 a.m. playing video games. They also need to wake up early enough to eat a good healthy breakfast. If they go to bed late, they're probably not going to feel like getting up early enough to eat. It all ties together. If athletes sleep better, they're going to feel better, study better, and perform better, both academically and athletically.

Supplementation is one of those "icing on the cake" issues. Most kids don't need to supplement their diets unless they're not eating enough healthy meals and snacks. A general recommendation from me would be for kids to take a multivitamin and fish oil to get essential fatty acids. Those are the top two. Number three would be some sort of protein supplement because kids in general don't get enough protein. They're not getting enough vitamins and minerals from their food, and hardly any of them are getting enough omega-3 fatty acids in their diet. Those three are essential for most kids to incorporate daily.

The third S, stretching, will help alleviate muscle soreness and those minor aches and pains. If something hurts, it's usually because those muscles are tight. So stretching, sleep, and supplementation are going to help you recover faster. A faster recovery means improved performance.

CHAPTER EIGHT
# Troubleshooting

In this chapter, I'm going to answer some of the most common questions I hear about training that we've haven't discussed already. I hope that this information will help you in making the decision to put your young athlete into a good, safe, effective training program.

## "WHAT HAPPENS IF MY SON OR DAUGHTER GETS INJURED DURING SPORTS? CAN THEY STILL TRAIN?"

Absolutely! They can train regardless of what the injury is. I always tell athletes to keep a positive mindset, no matter what the circumstances. So often, if somebody is injured, they automatically say, "Well, that's it. I can't do anything because I'm injured. I have to rest. I have to sit and not do anything."

In my opinion, that's the wrong way to go about it. You should always focus on what you can do as opposed to what you can't do. There's always a way to work around injuries. I don't care what the injury is, unless you just had surgery that requires you to have complete bed rest. For most sport injuries, you can still train around them and get good results.

You don't want to get out of shape, even when you're injured. You want to maintain the physical preparation you built up as much as you can. You are allowing the injury to heal while you are training. It will actually help speed up the recovery process when training is conducted properly. It's just a matter of being creative and having the desire to do it.

## "WHAT ABOUT IN-SEASON TRAINING? SHOULD YOUNG ATHLETES TRAIN DURING THE SEASON?"

Yes, in-season training is very important. You've got to look at it like this—you're driving from point A to point B. You're in the middle of this long trip, and you've prepared for it and gassed up and gotten your oil changed and ... suddenly you stop in the middle of the trip because you feel like you've gone far enough. Never mind about getting to point B. You're just done.

That's sort of like what ending your training during the season is like. You're going to lose a lot of what you built up if you stop training. In-season training is very important to maintain the qualities and the skills you've built up from the long off-season. If you just stop training completely, a lot of that strength and speed that took forever to build up is just going to go away. And it goes away very quickly if you don't train. Even if you're only training one to two times a week, it's still enough to maintain what you've built up. And then once the season's over, you're going to have a better transition back into training mode versus if you stop completely. Then you'll have to start all over again. And the cycle continues. It's much easier and more beneficial to keep training, even if the frequency of training has to be modified. One to two times per week is better than nothing at all. You just have to make it a habit, a lifestyle. It can't just be a six-week program.

## "HOW OLD DOES MY CHILD HAVE TO BE TO START TRAINING?"

We have athletes as young as 8 years old in our youth program. I think that is a pretty good age to start for most kids. Young athletes have to be able to take direction, though, and some kids aren't ready to do that until they're 9 or 10. So it depends on the kid, if they can handle direction or not. If they can listen and follow direction and be focused in this sort of environment—and enjoy the process—then for sure they're ready for it. But if you ask me to put a number on it, I would say age 8 or 9 is a good starting age for most kids. They're going to be training only one to two times per week at that age anyway. It's really not a huge time or mental commitment for them at that point.

## "SHOULD MY YOUNG FEMALE ATHLETE ENGAGE IN STRENGTH TRAINING?"

Absolutely! Female athletes should be strength training year-round, regardless of what sport they play. Not only will they build up speed and power, but they'll also build up a healthy body image and lots of self-confidence. It's very important for girls and young women to understand that they can be strong, that they can be fit, that they can be their own person. They can kick butt, too! Strength training is absolutely essential for your female athlete.

## "WILL STRENGTH TRAINING HELP MY SON OR DAUGHTER RUN FASTER?"

Yes, indeed. The potential for speed is dramatically increased when an athlete has a higher level of overall body strength. Whatever their body weight is, if they're stronger per pound of body weight, then they're going to run faster than an athlete of equal weight who is not as strong, who can't produce as much force. Not only that, but a stronger athlete can absorb more force, too. So the stronger they are, the longer they can hold sprint form, and the longer they can go without getting tired. That's extremely important because we can teach all the running technique we want, but if the athlete can't hold sprint form, if he or she can't get in the right positions or have the right technique, it doesn't do us any good. This isn't to say speed work isn't important – because it is! But there has to be focus on building up the necessary basic qualities first before we can really dig deeper and get into the more specific speed training to see any sort of long-lasting benefit. So yes, strength training will definitely improve your child's speed.

## "WHAT IF MY CHILD JUST DECIDES TO WORK OUT ON HIS OR HER OWN?"

You never know; they might get better, they might not. Most likely they will not. Let's say a student is struggling with math in school, for example. He's not going to try to learn it on his own; you're going to find a tutor for him. Or let's say your daughter wants to learn how to drive. You don't just hand her the keys and say, "Go to it." You take her to a driving instructor, or at the very least, teach her yourself.

It's the same with training. A young athlete might be able to do it on his or her own, but the chances of doing it the right way with the right program are pretty slim. Especially when you keep safety in mind, you need to have your son or daughter train with a professional. That is an essential element of keeping them in a good program over the long term.

## "MY CHILD TAKES WEIGHT TRAINING IN SCHOOL. ISN'T THAT ENOUGH?"

Unfortunately, it's not. Most kids that we see who

take weight training in school are not working with a teacher or a coach who has a lot of experience in the subject. The programming is not ideal. The class is usually for a large group of students, and everybody is different with varying abilities. It's just not something that should be a cookie-cutter program. The large class size also means that kids are more likely to socialize than work hard, and they're not going to get quality time using the weights. The teacher simply can't oversee 60 kids doing weight training all at once. In an ideal weight room setting, it's highly structured and closely supervised to produce the best results possible with qualified experts. That's just the facts.

## "WHAT IF MY SON OR DAUGHTER DOES NOT STRENGTH TRAIN?"

Every athlete has that decision to make, and every decision has its consequence. No matter what you decide, it's ultimately your call. If you don't strength train, you're leaving a lot of potential on the table. It's a matter of what you could have done if you had gone into a program. I don't want any young athlete to look back and have regrets. If your child doesn't participate in a proper program that's structured to achieve the best results, then he or she may not reach full potential as an athlete. There are so many advantages to strength training and working in a structured, disciplined program. A young athlete's body should be able to work hard and achieve its full potential, and these kids are at a time in their lives where it's ideal to pursue a program like this. They can choose to do the hard work now, or they can play catch-up later.

Athletes write their own stories with every decision they make, from now until the time their athletic careers are finished. I tell these kids, "You are the director of your own movie. You are the writer of your own story." The parents play a special role with the success of their child. Every decision can affect the ultimate outcome of how successful kids are and where they end up. Together with the proper coaching, programming, and environment and the commitment from both the athletes and the parents, you create a winning recipe for success.

I want everybody who reads this book who is not participating in a strength and conditioning program to know that you're leaving a lot of potential unfulfilled. That's how I honestly feel. You've got to make that call. We're here to guide you in the right direction and provide you with the best possible solution to maximize your son or daughter's potential as an athlete.

For those of you reading who have a son or daughter participating in a strength & conditioning program, know that the work they are putting in is laying the foundation for success.

Focus on the process, not so much the outcomes, and you will have success in all of your athletic endeavors. When in doubt, always remember to take things one day or one session at a time and don't be afraid to reach out to someone who can help guide you in the right direction.

If you need to run faster, jump higher, and get stronger for your sport, CTS can help. Call us directly at (707) 738-0190 to discuss how we can help your son or daughter become the best athlete they can be.

**JOHN CORTESE**